BIG MACHINES

Cranes

David and Penny Glover

FRANKLIN WATTS
LONDON • SYDNEY

This edition 2007

Franklin Watts
338 Euston Road, London, NW1 3BH

Franklin Watts Australia
Level 17/207 Kent Street, Sydney, NSW 2000

Copyright © Franklin Watts 2004

Series editor: Sarah Peutrill
Designer: Richard Langford
Art director: Jonathan Hair
Reading consultant: Margaret Perkins, Institute of Education, University of Reading

Picture credits: Colin Beere/Topham: 7b. Ian Britton/Freefoto: 23. David Frazier/Image Works/Topham: 21b. Tiffany M Hermon/Image Works/Topham: 19. Image Works/Topham: 8t, 17t. PA/Topham: 9, 15. Picturepoint/Topham: front cover, 6, 13t, 20. Joel W. Rogers/Corbis: 22. Joe Sohm/Image Works/Topham: 21t. Courtesy of Street Crane Co Ltd: 7t, 8b, 12, 14. Courtesy of Terex Cranes Ltd: 13b, 18. Every attempt has been made to clear copyright. Should there be any inadvertent omission, please apply to the publisher for rectification.

With particular thanks to Street Crane and Terex for permission to use their photos.

Dewey number: 621.8'73
ISBN: 978 0 7496 7809 8

Printed in Malaysia

Franklin Watts is a division of Hachette Children's Books, an Hachette Livre UK company.

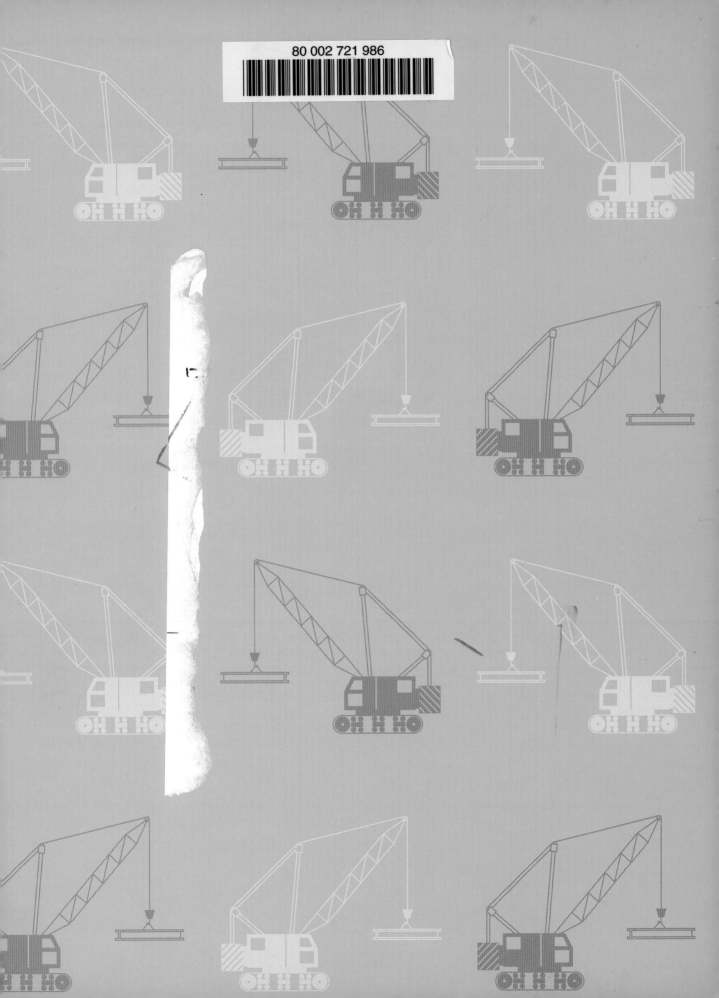

Contents

Lifting machines

Cranes are big lifting machines. They lift heavy girders and blocks on building sites. Giant cranes on dock sides can load or unload a whole ship in just a few hours.

There are many types of crane, but they all lift loads.

Tower cranes lift materials at a building site.
▼

A dock-side crane lifts a boat into the water.

This crane lifts an escalator into a building.

Lifting hook

A crane picks up its load with a hook. The hook passes through a loop of chain called the sling, which goes around the load.

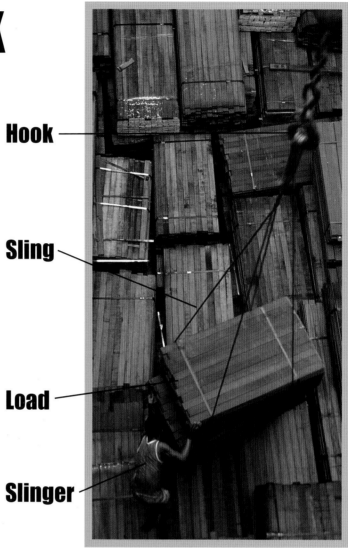

Hook

Sling

Load

Slinger

▲ The slinger hooks the load onto the sling.

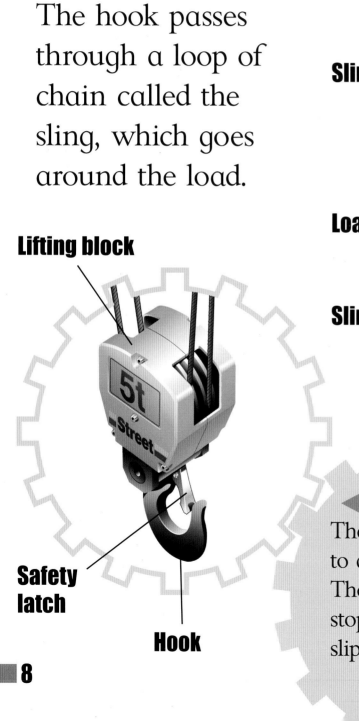

Lifting block

5t

Street

Safety latch

Hook

◄ The hook is attached to a lifting block. The safety latch stops the load from slipping off the hook.

Some cranes have two hooks for lifting awkward loads.

Hanging the load from two hooks helps to balance it as it goes up and down.

Pulleys and cables

The hook hangs from the crane's cable. The cable moves up or down to raise or lower the load.

Steel cable

The cable is very stong. This is because it is made from steel wire.

The cable runs over pulleys. Pulleys are wheels with grooves. The cable fits into the groove so it can wind up and down smoothly. The pulleys turn as the cable moves around them.

Cable

Pulley

Lifting block

A pulley inside the lifting block turns as the cable winds up and down.

The jib

The crane's long arm is called the jib. Like a fishing rod, it helps the driver to place the hook exactly where it is needed, then lift the load high above the ground.

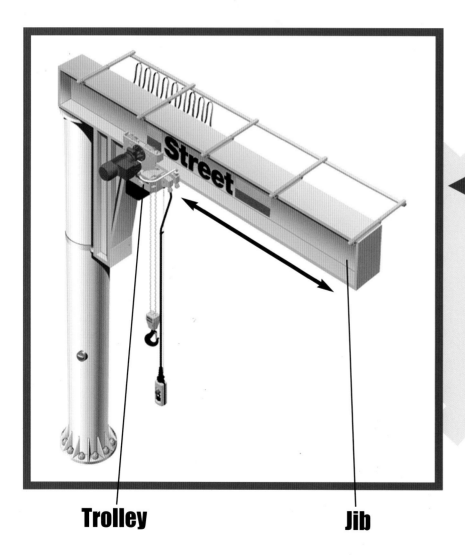

The jib on a tower crane points out sideways from the top of the tower. A trolley moves along the jib to carry the load from place to place.

Trolley

Jib

The jibs on these cranes are very big so they can carry huge loads.

A mobile crane jib points up at an angle.

The driver can extend (lengthen) the jib, then swing it around into position.

The winch

The winch winds the cable up and down. It is turned by an electric motor. The cable wraps around the winch like cotton around a huge cotton reel.

Electric motor

Winch

Street

Street

50t

Turning the winch one way winds the cable up to lift the load. Turning the winch the other way lets the cable out, lowering the load again.

The main winch lifts the load. It is called the hoist.

Hoist

Other winches pull cables to move different parts of the crane.

In the cab

Cab

Ladder

The crane driver sits in the cab. The cab turns with the jib so that the driver can always see the load.

◀ The cab on this crane is high up, just under the jib. The driver has to climb a ladder inside the tower to reach it.

BIG FACT

The cab on a tall tower crane may be more than 100 metres above the ground.

This crane driver can easily see the load and the slingers below.

Inside the cab the driver uses buttons and levers to work the crane.

The driver uses different levers to move the jib and raise or lower the hook.

Keeping steady

Imagine standing on one leg holding a heavy weight. You could easily topple over. The same thing can happen to a tall crane if it is not balanced properly.

A tower crane is kept steady by a weight on the side of the tower that is opposite to the load.

Balance weight   Tower   Load

◄ The weight can be moved to balance the jib. When the load is big, the weight is moved away from the tower. When the load is smaller, the weight is moved towards the tower.

A mobile crane puts down legs before it begins to lift. The legs help to keep it steady.

Leg

A mobile crane's legs are used to steady it before lifting a house.

Different cranes

Different kinds of crane are used in different places.

This crawler crane moves on caterpillar tracks. It carries heavy loads around building sites and quarries.

Caterpillar tracks

This huge crane is called an overhead crane. It is moving a load onto a container ship.

Beam

Trolley

Load

The hooks hang from a trolley that moves to and fro along the beam.

This crane is on an oil rig. It runs on tracks along the platform and lifts loads onto the rig.

Giant cranes

The most powerful cranes in the world are giant derrick cranes. They can lift loads of more than 1,000 tonnes - the weight of 100 elephants!

BIG FACT

The K-10,000 tower crane is the world's tallest crane. It can lift loads 120 metres into the air.

▲ This giant derrick crane is helping to build a skyscraper.

The Asian Hercules II is one of the biggest floating cranes in the world.

▲

The Asian Hercules II lifts a bridge into place across a river.

Make it yourself

Make a model derrick crane.

You will need:

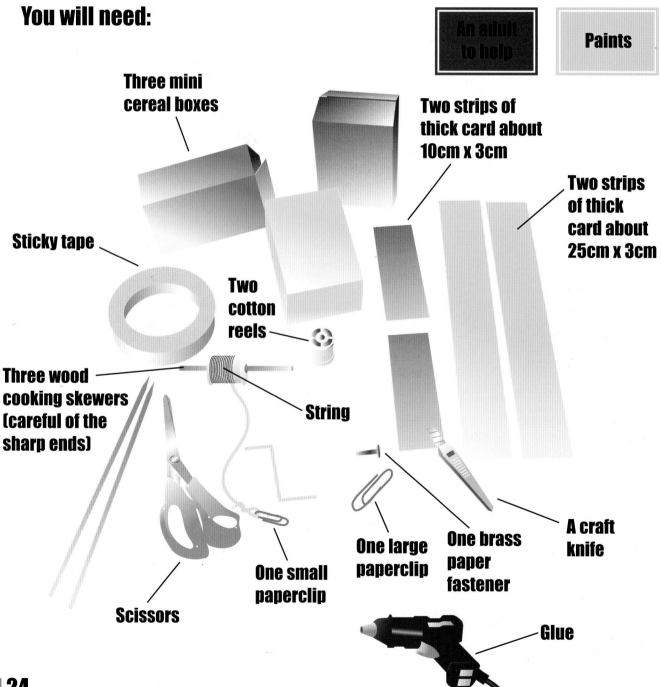

An adult to help

Paints

Three mini cereal boxes

Two strips of thick card about 10cm x 3cm

Two strips of thick card about 25cm x 3cm

Sticky tape

Two cotton reels

String

Three wood cooking skewers (careful of the sharp ends)

Scissors

One small paperclip

One large paperclip

One brass paper fastener

A craft knife

Glue

SAFETY! An adult must help you with the cutting and sticking.

1. Glue two cereal boxes together to make the base of the crane.

Use the paper fastener to fix the third box to the base to make the cab. The cab should turn on the base.

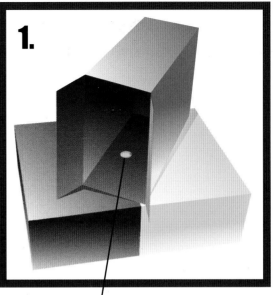

Paper fastener

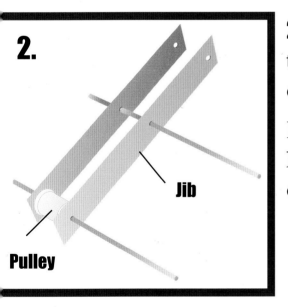

2.

Jib

Pulley

2. Ask an adult to make small holes at the centre, and at both ends, of the long card strips.

Push a wood skewer through the centre holes. Pass the top skewer through a cotton reel. This is the pulley.

3. Pass the bottom skewer through the cab to fix the jib in place.

Trim the skewers to the right length on either side of the jib.

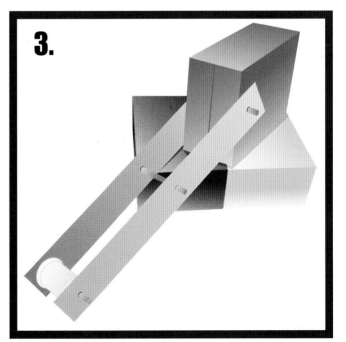

3.

4. Make a small hole at the back of the cab. Raise the jib at an angle, and support it by tying string between its centre skewer and the hole.

Push a skewer through the other reel. Leave about 2 cm of skewer on either side. Fix it to the reel with tape or glue so that it will not spin. This is your winch.

Make holes for the skewer in the short card strips. Push them on either side of the winch. The skewer will spin in the holes.

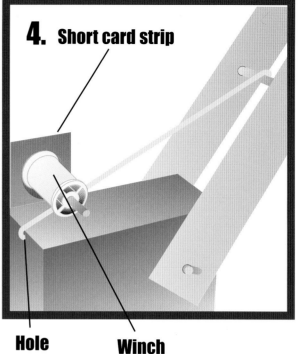

4. Short card strip

Hole   Winch

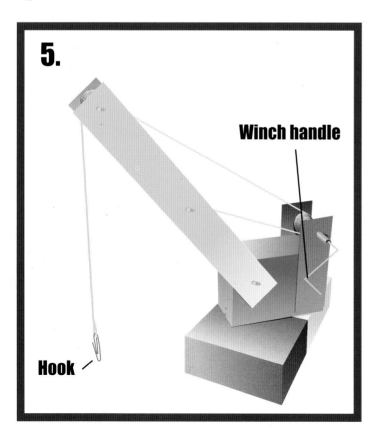

5.

Winch handle

Hook

5. Glue the card strips to either side of the cab.

Make a winch handle by bending the large paper clip. Tape it in place as shown.

Wrap string around the winch and pass it over the pulley to make your cable.

Make a hook from the small paper clip and tie it on.

Use your crane to lift a load.

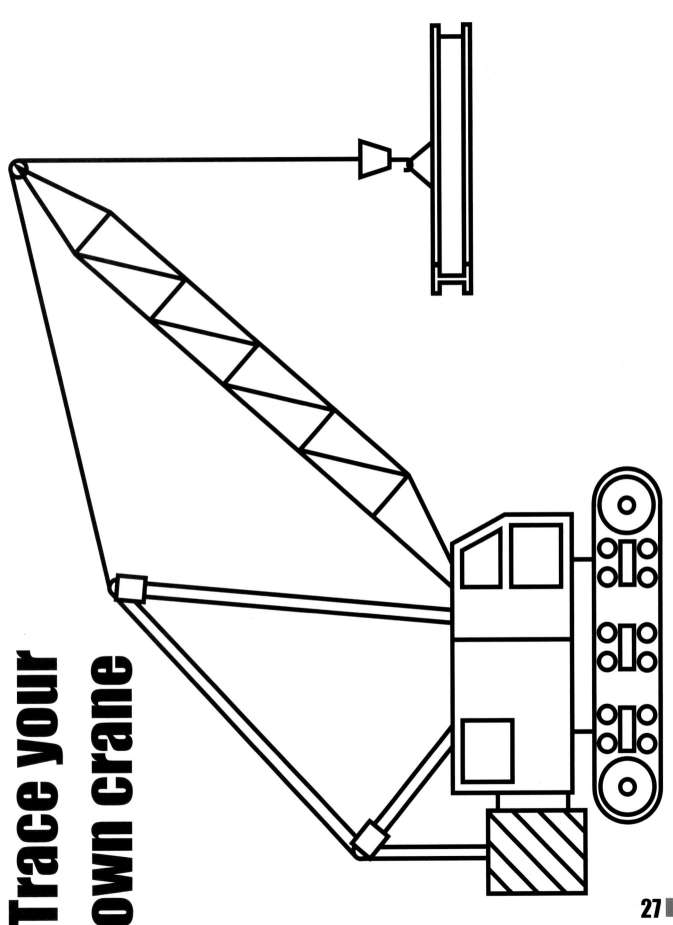

Trace your own crane

Crane words

cab

The part of the crane in which the driver sits.

cable

A strong steel rope.

derrick crane

A crane with a jib that points up at an angle.

girder

A large strong metal beam.

hoist

The main winch which winds the cable to lift the load.

hook

The curved piece of metal that hooks the load to the cable.

jib

A crane's main lifting arm.

lifting block

The metal block to which the hook is fixed.

load

The thing that the crane lifts.

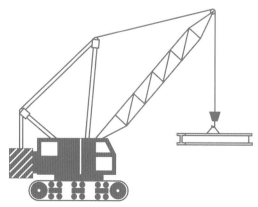

pulley
A wheel with a grooved rim.

safety latch
A metal finger that stops the cable slipping out of the hook.

sling
A loop of chain or cable in which the load rests.

slinger
The person who hooks the load onto the crane.

tower crane
A crane with a jib that points out sideways.

trolley
A block that moves along a tower crane jib to put the load over the right place.

winch
A drum or reel that winds the cable up and down.

Index

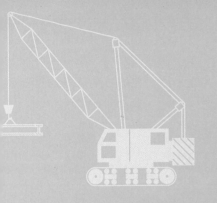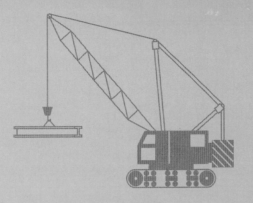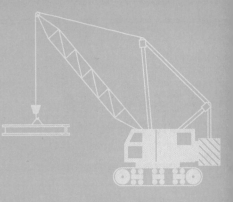
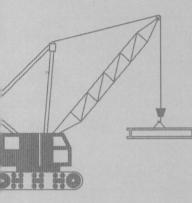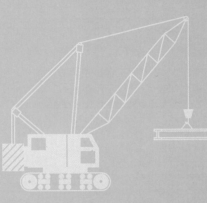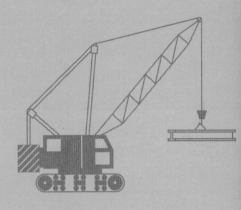
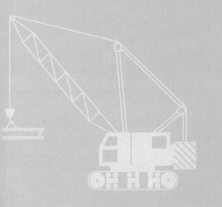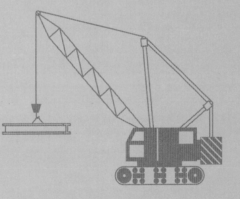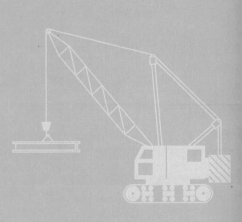
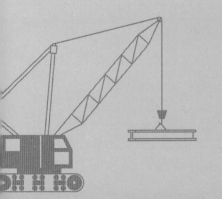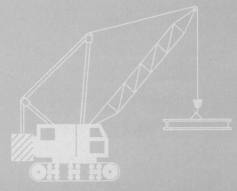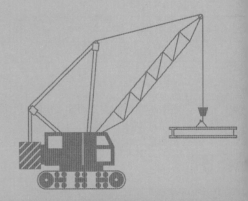